Origami PLANES

Origami PLANES

15 step-by-step projects to make, plus techniques

mari ono

CICO BOOKS

Published in 2026 by CICO Books
An imprint of Ryland Peters & Small Ltd
20–21 Jockey's Fields 1452 Davis Bugg Road
London WC1R 4BW Warrenton, NC 27589
www.rylandpeters.com
Email: euregulations@rylandpeters.com

Text and models in this book originally featured in *Fly Origami Fly*

10 9 8 7 6 5 4 3 2 1

A CIP record for this book is available from the British Library.
US Library of Congress CIP data has been applied for.

ISBN: 978-1-80065-642-0

Printed in China

Photography: Geoff Dann
Photography styling and illustration: Trina Dalziel

Assistant editor: Danielle Rawlings
Senior designer: Emily Breen
Art director: Sally Powell
Head of production: Patricia Harrington
Publishing manager: Carmel Edmonds

The authorised representative in the EEA is
Authorised Rep Compliance Ltd.,
Ground Floor. 71 Lower Baggot Street,
Dublin, D01 P593, Ireland
www.arccompliance.com

Safety note: Adults should supervise young children at all times when they are using scissors or glue.

CONTENTS

BASIC TECHNIQUES

The most basic skill of origami is folding paper precisely and creating strong, straight creases. This can be achieved through concentration and ensuring folded edges and corners match perfectly before firming up creases. To build up models, more complicated folds are needed to ensure the paper retains its shape.

MAKING FOLDS

Making the paper fold as crisply and evenly as possible is the key to making models that will look as the designs intend—it really is as simple as that.

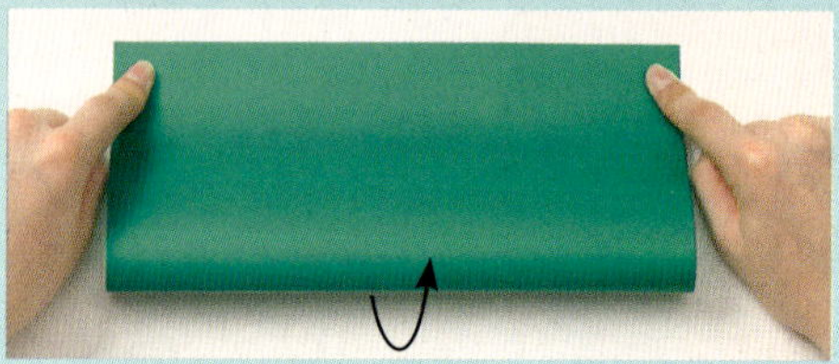

1 When you make a fold, ensure that the paper lies exactly where you want it, with the corners sitting exactly on top of each other.

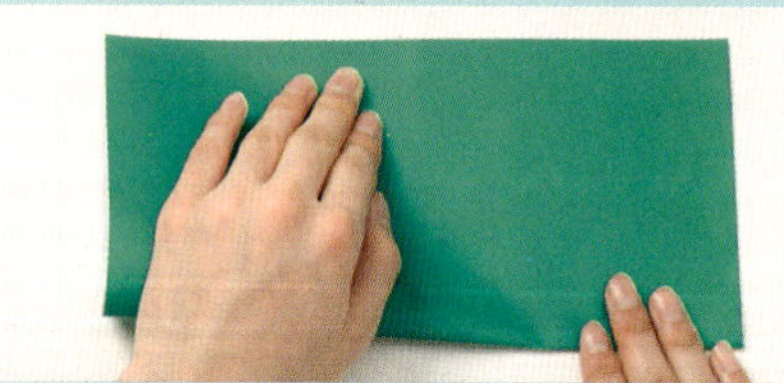

2 As you make the crease, be sure to keep the paper completely still so that the fold is perfectly true and straight.

3 Still holding the paper with your spare hand, use a ruler or perhaps the side of a pencil to press down the fold until it is as flat as possible.

OPENING FOLDS

Sometimes you will need to open out a crease and refold the paper so that it lies in a new shape, as in the triangle fold shown here.

1 Lift the flap to be opened out and begin pulling the two sides apart.

2 As the space widens, you will need to be sure that the far point folds true, so use a pencil to gently prise the paper open.

DIFFICULTY RATING

The complexity of each project in the book has been calculated on a scale of 1–3. Level 1 is the simplest, while level 3 requires the use of some complex folding techniques. If you allow yourself to gain confidence gradually you will soon be successfully creating the most intricate of designs.

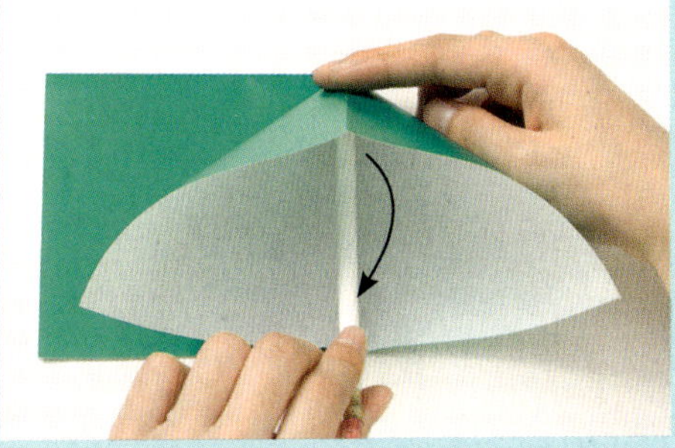

3 As the two corners separate, the top point drops forward and the two edges open out to become one.

4 Press down the new creases to make the two new angled sides of the triangle.

KEY TO ARROWS

FOLDING DIRECTION
Fold the entire paper over in the direction of the arrow.

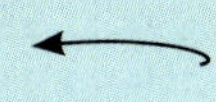

MAKE A CREASE
Fold the paper in the direction of the arrow, then unfold again to make a crease.

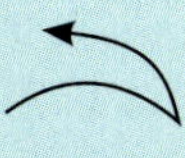

OPEN OUT
Open out and refold the paper in the direction shown.

TURN OVER
Turn the paper over without changing the top and bottom edges.

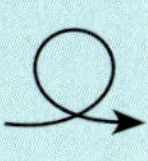

CHANGE THE POSITION
Rotate the paper 90 degrees or 180 degrees in the direction of the arrows.

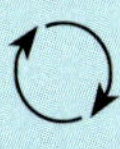

INSERT
Insert the paper in the direction of the arrow.

VALLEY FOLD
Fold the paper in the direction of the arrow to make a trough.

MOUNTAIN FOLD
Fold the paper in the direction of the arrow to make a peak.

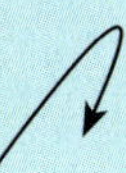

INSIDE FOLD

Use this technique to surround one part of the sheet of paper with the rest, enclosing much of the fold between the outer parts of the sheet beneath the fold line.

1 Make a fold, here from corner to corner, and then turn down one corner at the intended final angle below the main crease.

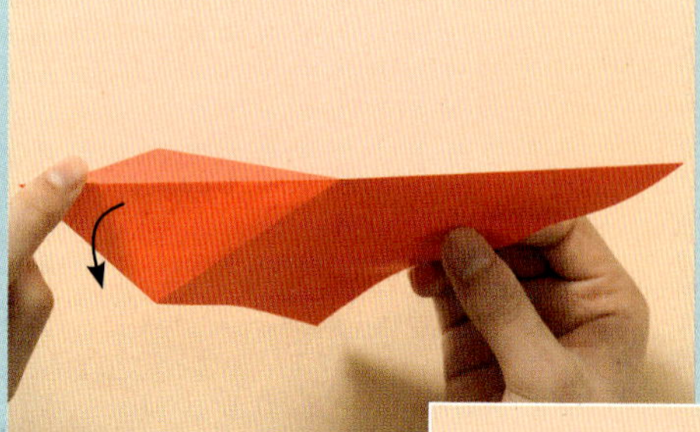

2 Lift the sheet and open out the corner that was folded over then push down the outer point of the edge, reversing the crease.

3 When the sheet is flattened the folded corner will be inside the paper with the reverse of the design showing.

CUTTING PAPER

Instead of using scissors, you can get an accurate cut with a paper cutter.

1 Mark the start and end points of your intended cut with an awl.

2 Set the metal edge of the ruler on the points marked in step 1. Cut along the ruler using the paper cutter. Be certain that the tip of the cutter follows the edge of the ruler.

OUTSIDE FOLD

Use this technique to enclose the majority of a sheet with one folded corner, pushing the folded tip over the main crease line.

1 Make a fold across the paper, turning the tip over and beyond the fold line.

2 Open out the sheet and fold the corner of the paper up and backward, reversing the creases.

3 When the sheet is flattened, the folded corner will be outside the paper with the reverse of the design showing.

FLYING SCHOOL

All of the planes and gliders will fly, though there are different ways to launch them. Follow the instructions below and then practice to find the best way to achieve a long flight.

CENTRAL BODY PLANES

Many of the planes are folded so that they have central bodies. Grip the plane between your thumb and forefinger to launch.

Ross-17—page 28

Vertical Tail—page 44

Sunlight—page 18

To achieve really long flights with these central body planes it can be helpful to throw the model high into the air. Use as much power as you can and practice to find the angle that works best.

1 Start by holding the plane low next to your ankles with your knees bent.

2 As you raise the plane lift your body as well.

3 Point the plane high into the sky and swivel your body to gain as much power as possible when you let go.

NO BODY PLANES

Some of the planes do not have bodies to grasp so they are more difficult to launch a significant distance. All of them will fly with a flick of the wrist.

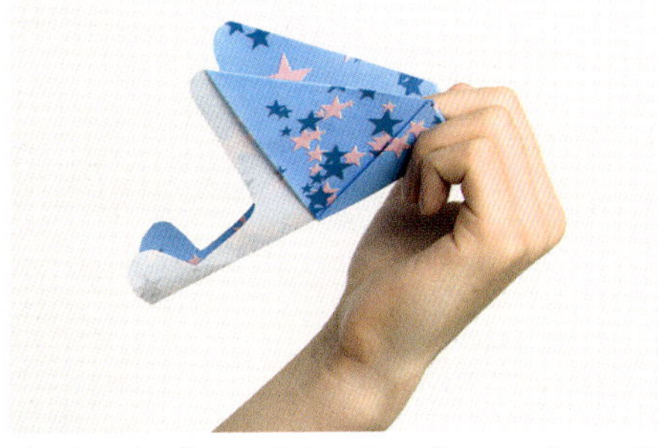

1 Grip the front of the plane from underneath with the tips of your fingers.

2 Flick your hand forward from the wrist to launch.

3 Ensure your fingers end up pointing in the direction you want the plane to fly. The flying Brick (see page 53) should also be launched in this way.

Star Light—page 14

Brick—page 53

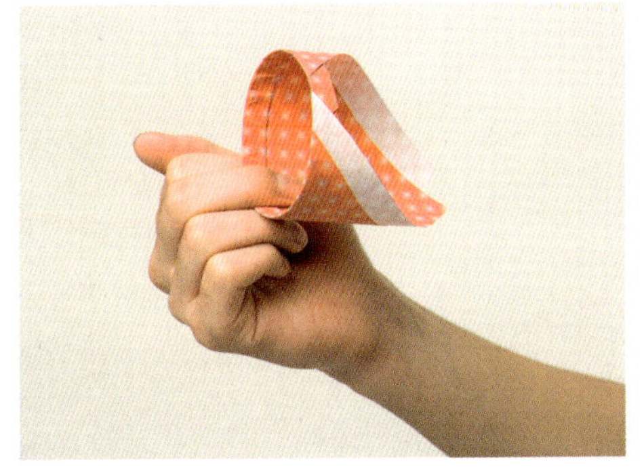

UNIQUELY SHAPED GLIDERS

Some gliders, such as the Magic Ring (see page 12), look like they shouldn't fly at all. Hold it with your fingers and throw it forward to see it fly as far as any plane!

01 MAGIC RING

The magic of this project is that it flies extraordinarily well. The trick is to get much of the paper's weight into the narrow band that forms the central axis. This gives the ring natural rotation, which allows every throw to be straight. Once you have mastered the knack, your friends will be amazed by this fantastic flyer.

Skill rating ● ● ●

You will need
1 sheet of A5 (8¼ x 6in/21 x 15cm) paper

1 Find the center point by folding the paper in half twice then opening out.

2 Fold the paper diagonally through the center point so that the creases end up directly on top of one another to ensure that the sides are parallel.

3 Now turn the bottom edge up, using the outer points of the object as the crease points before rolling the bottom up again, halving the width of the flap just made. Next turn over the bottom flap once more.

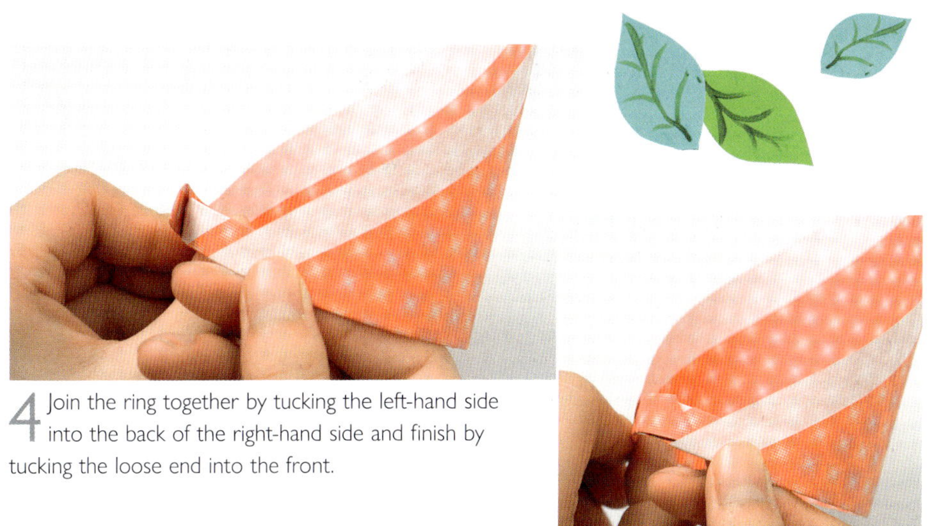

4 Join the ring together by tucking the left-hand side into the back of the right-hand side and finish by tucking the loose end into the front.

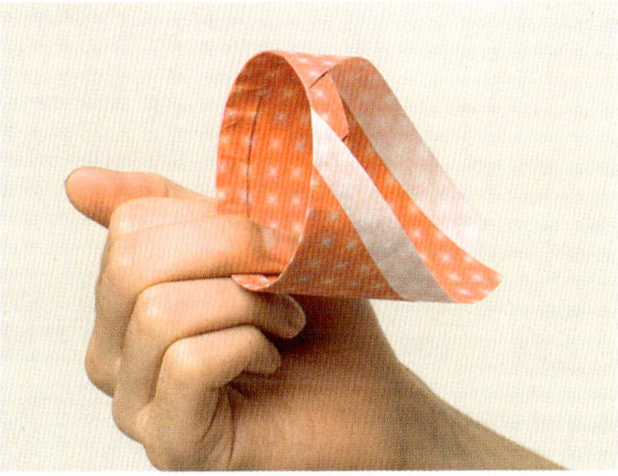

5 Throw the ring by holding it from underneath with your middle finger and flicking it forward.

02 STAR LIGHT

In Japan, the Star Light is called the "Swallow Plane" as it closely resembles the bird's swooping shape and flies with the same easy style as well. It does not have a body like most paper planes and flies in a unique way as it is thrown by a flick of your fingers out of the back of your hand. With practice the Star Light will fly as well as any plane.

Skill rating ● ● ●

You will need

1 sheet of A5 (8¼ x 6in/21 x 15cm) paper

Scissors

1 First, fold the paper in half lengthwise and open out to make a crease. Next fold the corners of one end across to the other side of the paper opening both out to make diagonal creases.

2 Fold the right-hand end of the paper over, using the crossing point of the diagonal creases as the marker for the fold.

3 Fold the corners into the center using the diagonal creases made earlier as the fold lines.

4 Open out the last folds and lift the nearest corner, taking it across to the other side of the paper so that the flap opens out before refolding it to form a triangle.

5 Fold the far point of the triangle back over to the near side of the object.

6 Lift the far point, opening out the flap and folding it toward you, forming another triangle.

7 Fold the top flap back over so that there is one flap on each side of the object.

8 Fold the corners of both top flaps over so that the corners meet at the object's end point.

9 Fold the sides of the central diamond across the center so that they meet along the center line.

10 Lift the paper and use scissors to cut along the center line from the tip to the point at which the two folds made in the last step meet.

11 Lift the top flaps and gently open them out with a finger or a pencil, then turn back each side of the nose and tuck them into the holes until the crease is flush.

12 Turn the object over and fold it in half along the central crease.

13 Use the scissors to cut out the shape of the wings and tail.

03 SUNLIGHT

The Sunlight is one of the fastest and most stable airplane designs. Its wide wing cuts through the wind, allowing it to fly straight and true, covering a good distance. Extend the duration of the flight even further by throwing it high up into the air. If you like, you can use a larger sheet of rectangular paper to make a bigger plane—which should also fly farther.

Skill rating ● ● ●

You will need
1 sheet of A5 (8¼ x 6in/21 x 15cm) paper

1 Fold lengthwise to make a crease then open out and fold the corners at one end into the center. Now fold the tip back so that the point lies at the point where the corners meet and make a crease.

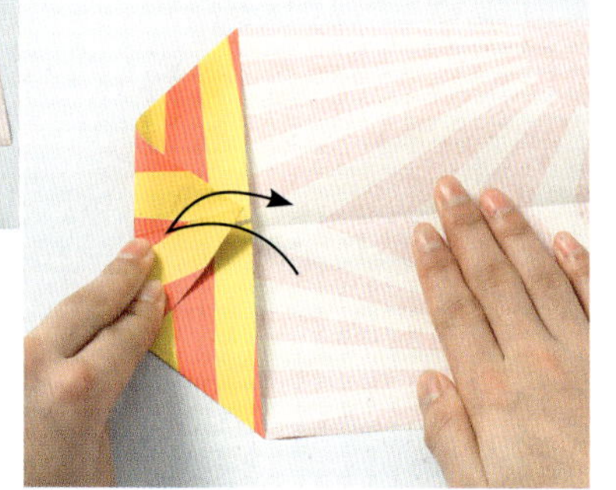

2 Turn the nose back and open out one flap before turning the tip back in. This will begin to reverse the folds of the flap.

ゴー

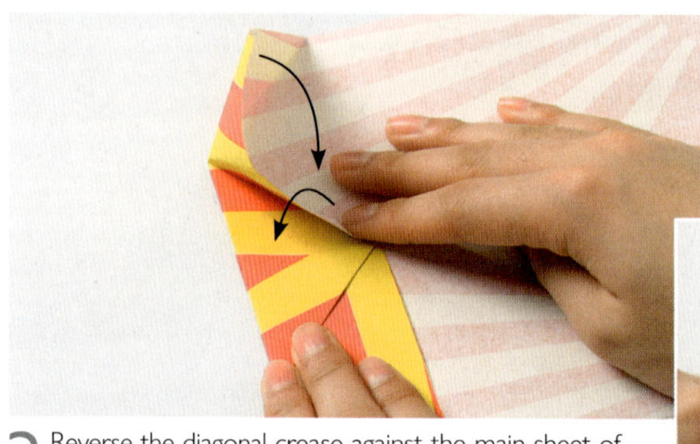

3 Reverse the diagonal crease against the main sheet of paper and bring the corner to lie on the central crease.

4 Open out the flap again to lift the nearer corner up then repeat the reversal of the creases and flatten.

5 Turn the whole paper over and fold the end back on itself.

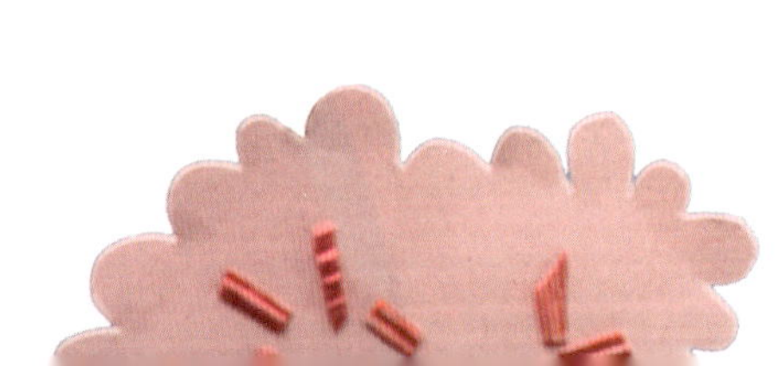

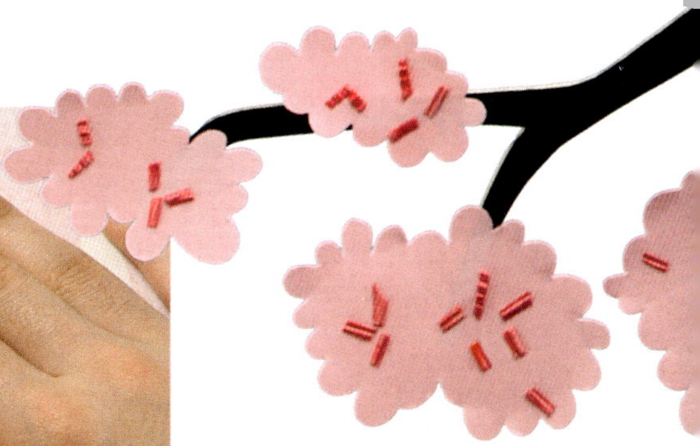

6 Turn the paper back over and turn the two folded corners in at a slight angle so that they meet on the central crease, leaving approximately 2in (5cm) of unturned paper at the far end.

7 Lift the paper up and fold the nearer half behind.

8 Fold down the wings, making the crease parallel with the base of the plane about halfway up the flat nose.

04 STAR STRIKE

The Star Strike is an airplane that is designed to fly fast and far, resembling a comet hurtling through outer space. Try playing with the Star Strike indoors in a large room, throwing it high up toward the ceiling where it can fly before gliding back down to earth.

Skill rating ● ● ●

You will need
1 sheet of A5 (8¼ x 6in/21 x 15cm) paper

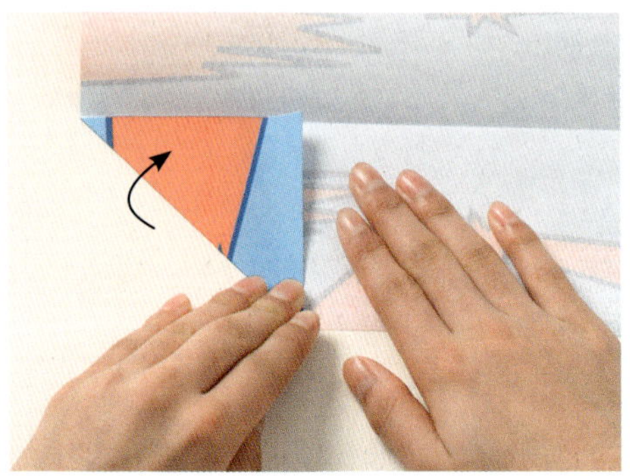

1 Fold the paper in half lengthwise and open out to leave a crease, then fold in the corners at one end to meet along the center line.

2 Fold in the angled edges so that they also meet along the central crease line.

3 Spin the paper round and fold back the tip, making a crease about 3in (7.5cm) in, ensuring that the tip just covers the point where the diagonal edges meet in the center of the paper.

4 Turn the paper over and open out the nose before folding it back on itself, making a crease approximately 2in (5cm) from the end.

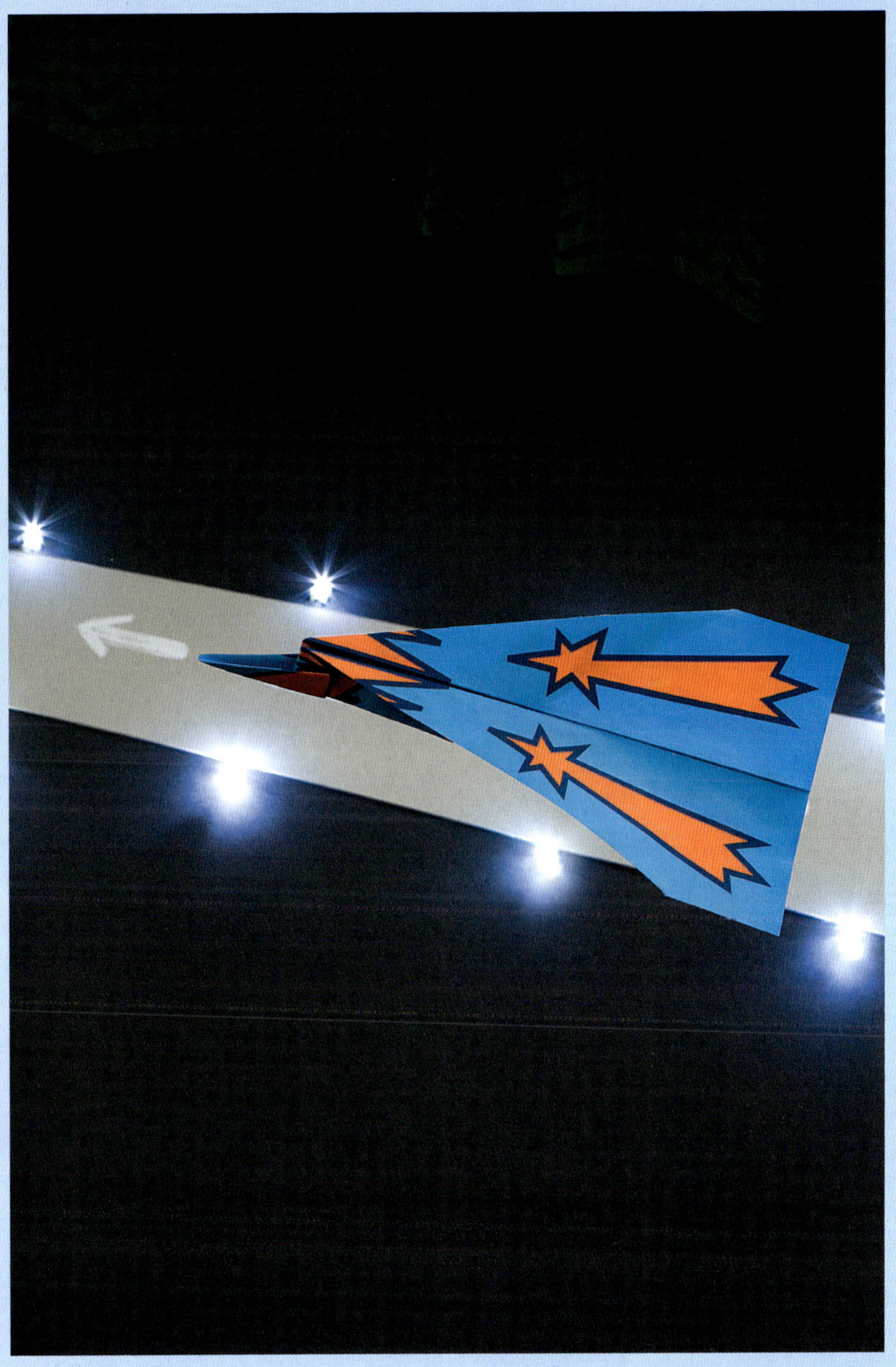

5 Turn the paper back over and fold up the nose using the two creases just made, then spin the object and fold it together along the central crease.

6 Fold down the wings with creases parallel to the base of the plane at the closest possible point to the nose.

05 ROARING FIRE

This airplane will light up the sky with its roaring fire. The flames will seem to glide behind the model as they flare across its wings. The large wing area, made by first folding the paper across its width, helps this airplane stay aloft. A powerful launch lifting it high into the air will see it blaze a trail across the sky.

Skill rating ● ● ●

You will need
1 sheet of A5 (8¼ x 6in/21 x 15cm) paper

1 Fold the paper in half widthwise and open out then turn the corners along one side in so that they meet on the central crease.

2 Next turn the tip back so that it sits on the far edge of the paper.

3 Fold the tip back so that the new crease lies halfway between the new edge and the original flaps.

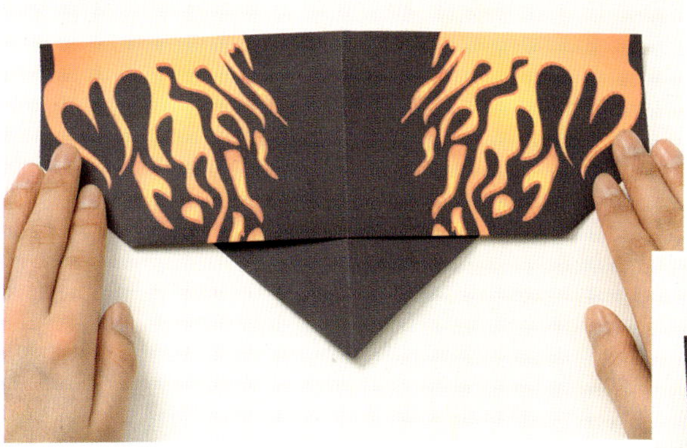

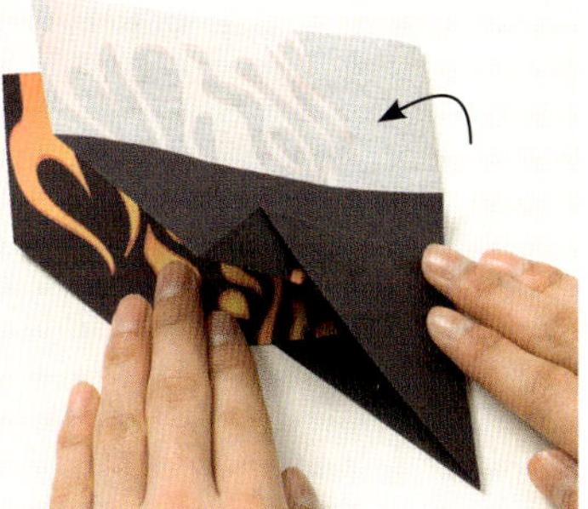

4 Turn the object over and fold in half along the central crease.

5 Place a ruler against the object to make a crisp, angled fold for the wing, starting at the end tip of the plane. Turn over and repeat on the other side to finish.

06 ROSS-17

This model flies best when the creases are thin and the folds sharp, which will stop the paper around the cockpit from becoming too thick and unwieldy. Take your time, though, as the folds you need to make this plane can be a little complex.

Skill rating ● ● ●

You will need
1 sheet of A5 (8¼ x 6in/21 x 15cm) paper

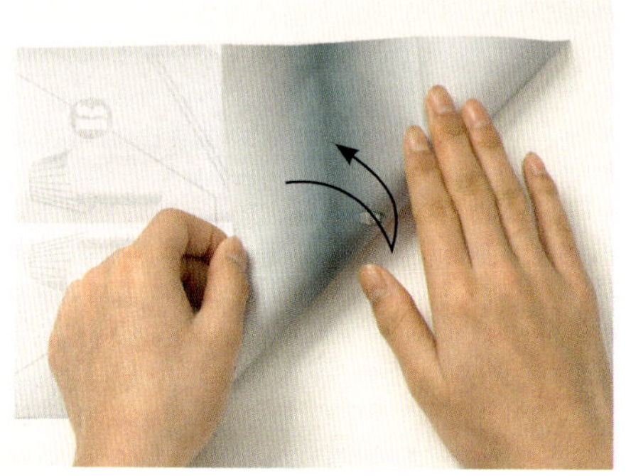

1 First, fold the paper along its length to make a crease and open out. Next fold one corner right across to the other side of the paper to make a diagonal crease and open out before repeating on the other side.

2 Turn over the end of the paper and make a fold where the diagonal creases cross.

3 Open out the fold and press the two sides together, reversing the horizontal crease so that the sides meet in the center and the end of the paper folds back down to create a triangle.

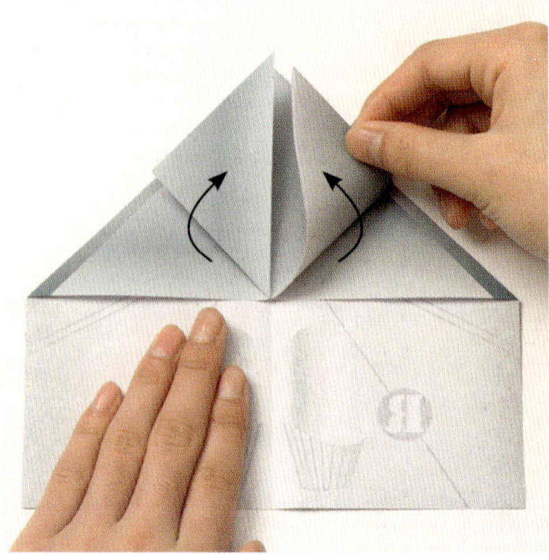

4 Fold back the top flap on each side so that the tips meet at the top of the paper and the edges lie up the central crease.

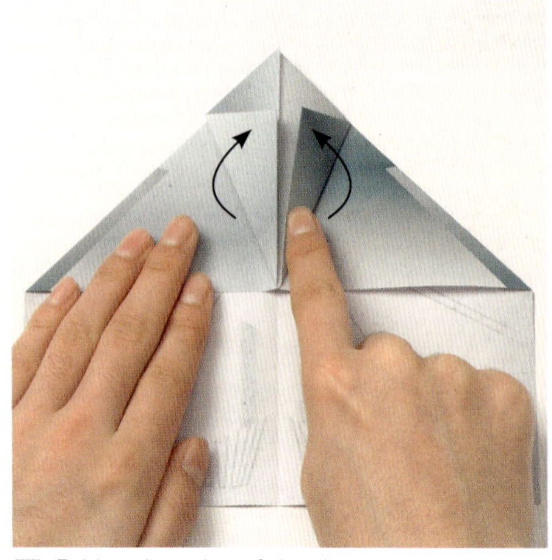

5 Fold in the sides of the diamond so that the edges meet along the middle with the flat edges of the triangles facing forward.

6 Turn back the top layers of the end point and tuck them into the flaps made in the previous step.

7 Lift up the sides of the diamond and fold the wing in underneath then let the diamond fall back into place.

8 Turn over the wing tips so that the points lie about ⅜in (1cm) apart directly along the bottom edge of the paper.

9 Form the wing tips into shape and press up the sides of the diamond so they are angled symmetrically to the plane.

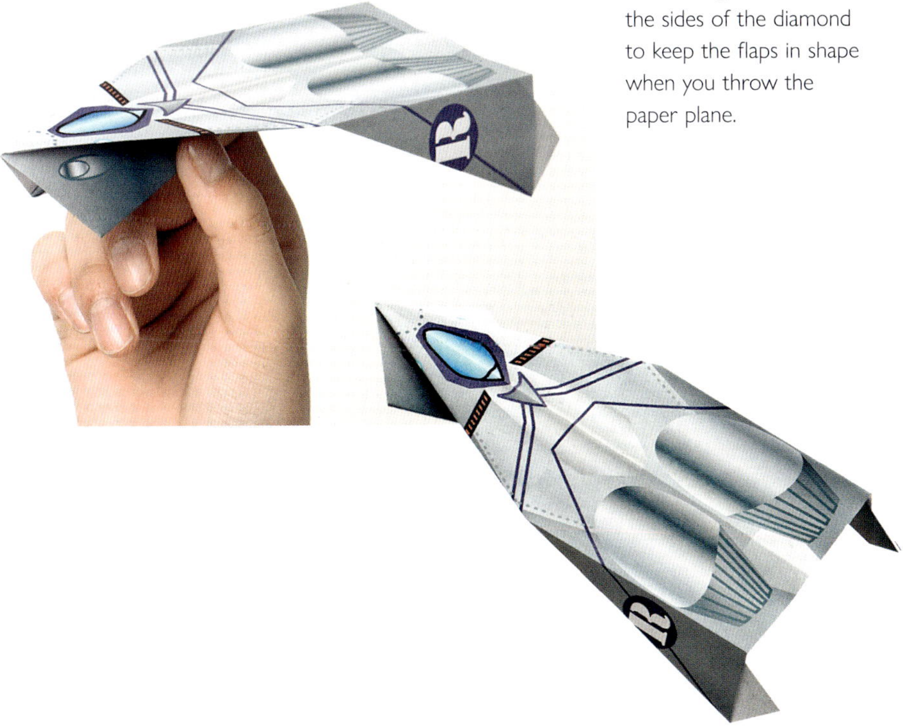

10 Place your first finger between the sides of the diamond to keep the flaps in shape when you throw the paper plane.

07 SCATTERED CLOUDS

The Scattered Clouds plane is a record breaker when it comes to flying long distances. To achieve the best results it is especially important to be accurate with the folds and make sure that every crease has been firmly pressed in place with a ruler. To fly high toward the sky, boost the length of your flight with a jump as you release the airplane into the air.

Skill rating 

You will need
1 sheet of A5 (8¼ x 6in/21 x 15cm) paper

1 Make a crease along the center of the paper then open out and fold the corners at one end into the middle. Next fold over the pointed end using the edges of the previous folds as guides.

2 Fold the top half of the paper forward along the central crease.

3 Turn up the bottom corner at a slight angle and make a crease.

4 Open out the paper and fold in the two corners along the creases made in the previous step.

5 Fold in the flaps so that the bottom edges meet along the central crease.

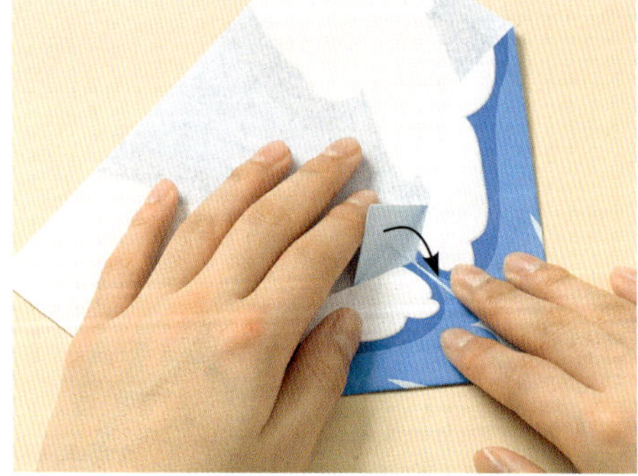

6 Fold forward the small triangle of paper sticking out from under the flaps so that it covers the flaps made in the previous step.

7 Turn the paper over and fold it together along the central crease, ensuring that the small triangle from the last step is still pointing forward.

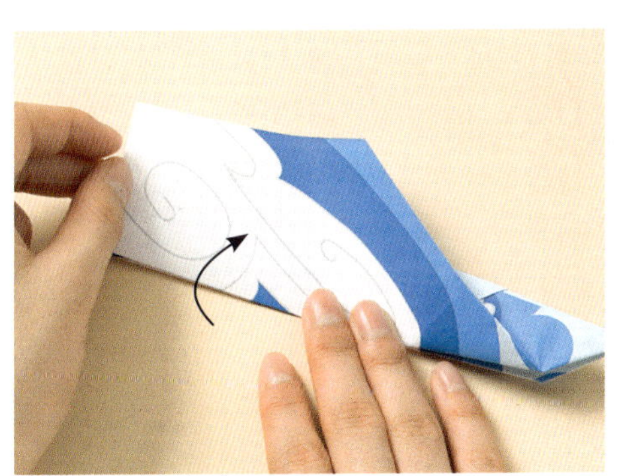

8 Turn over the wings with creases parallel to the base of the model to finish.

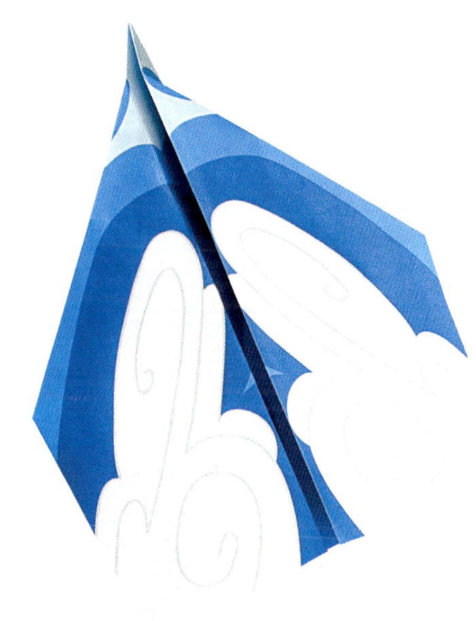

08 STEALTH JET

This jet is a classic in Japan and has been made by paper plane enthusiasts for generations. It is known as the "Squid Airplane" in Japan because its shape looks like a sea squid! Try applying some glue to the center of the plane—this will hold it together and help it to fly better.

Skill rating ● ● ●

You will need

1 sheet of A5 (8¼ x 6in/21 x 15cm) paper

Paper glue

1 Make a crease along the center of the paper by folding the colored sides together. Open out the sheet and fold two corners to meet along the central crease.

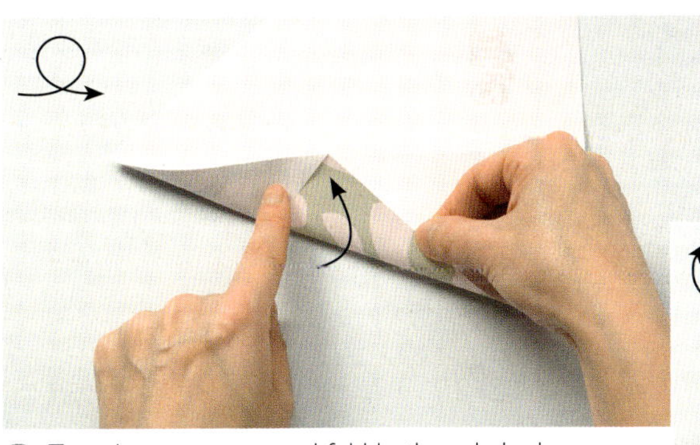

2 Turn the paper over and fold both angled edges in to meet along the central crease.

3 Lift up the object and open out the two loose flaps of paper at the pointed end.

4 Turn back the pointed end making the fold between the two outer points then lift the object and fold it in half along the central crease.

5 Lift the top flap forward to make the wing, making a straight fold about ½in (1.5cm) up from the bottom. Turn the paper over and repeat, then place a little paper glue in the space between the wings and press together.

09 THUNDERSTORM

The Thunderstorm is an exciting plane that will slice quickly through the air. With its large wing span it will fly far and true if you throw it with a bit of power up toward the sky. When you make this model plane take care to turn over the nose just enough so that the wings sit together without the need for any glue.

Skill rating ● ● ●

You will need

1 sheet of A5 (8¼ x 6in/21 x 15cm) paper

1 Fold the paper in half to make a crease then open it out again. Fold in the corners at one end to meet along the center line and then repeat, folding the angled sides so that they meet in the middle.

2 Fold back the end of the plane, making a crease about 5in (12.5cm) from the rear of the object.

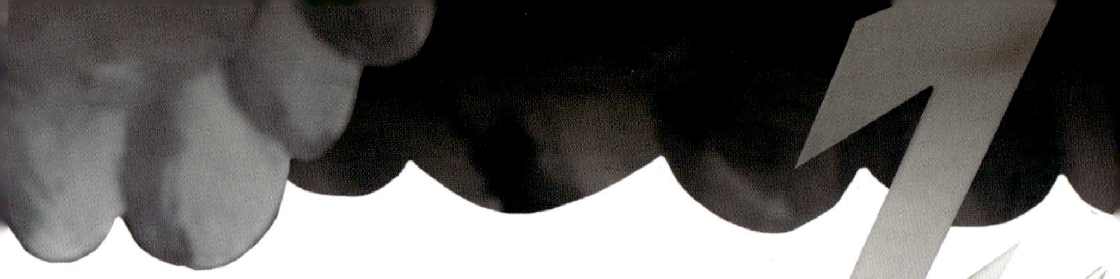

3 Turn the paper over and fold the back edges of the plane forward, angled so that they meet along the center line.

4 Turn the object over and fold it in half along the central crease.

5 Spin the object round and fold the tip of the nose across the main crease line then open out the paper.

6 Gently reverse the creases made when you turned over the nose and push the object back together so that the nose now points downward.

7 Fold the wings down, making the creases parallel to the bottom of the plane and starting just behind the turned nose.

10 VERTICAL TAIL

You can fine-tune The Vertical Tail to improve its performance. Experiment with different tail fin sizes, then test each one to find the one that flies farthest. You will immediately see the difference your adjustments can make to the paper plane's stability. The design on the paper is inspired by the model's flying ability and is based on the idea of a plane that can travel high into the atmosphere.

Skill rating ● ● ●

You will need
1 sheet of A5 (8¼ x 6in/21 x 15cm) paper

1 Make a crease down the middle of the paper then open it out and fold the corners at one end into the center.

2 Turn over the nose and fold the tip to about 1in (2.5cm) away from the edge of the paper, ensuring the fold is at right angles by placing the tip along the central crease.

3 Fold the corners into the center then fold the small triangle that remains visible back over to hold the folds in place.

4 Lift the paper up and fold the nearer half behind along the central crease.

5 Turn the paper over, then turn over the far end of the central crease at an angle then open out the plane and reverse the creases before closing up the plane once more.

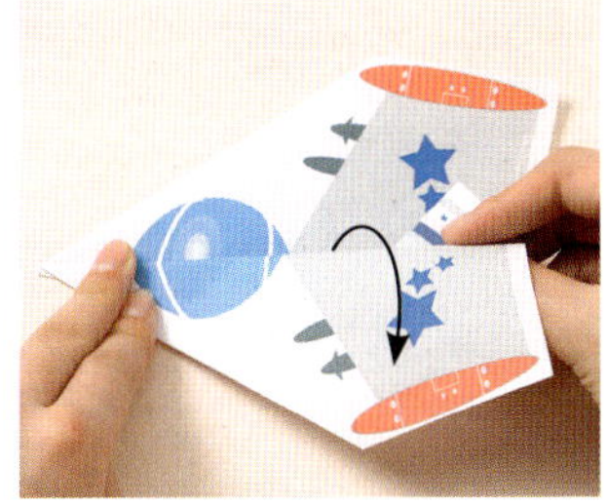

6 Turn down the wing leaving the body of the plane with a depth of no more than 3/8in (1cm) and repeat on the other side.

11 X-12

The X-12 has been designed to resemble one of the modern jet fighters seen in popular Japanese cartoons. Its sleek shape and polished look make it perfect for aerial assaults in the backyard. When you are flying your plane with friends, take care not to throw it straight toward them because the point is a bit sharp and a direct hit could hurt them!

Skill rating 

You will need
1 sheet of A5 (8¼ x 6in/21 x 15cm) paper

1 With the printed side upward fold the sheet of paper in half lengthwise. Next turn down both corners at one end before also turning over the angled edges.

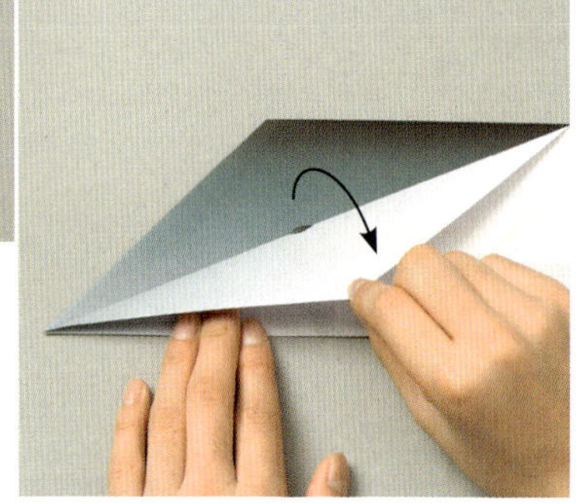

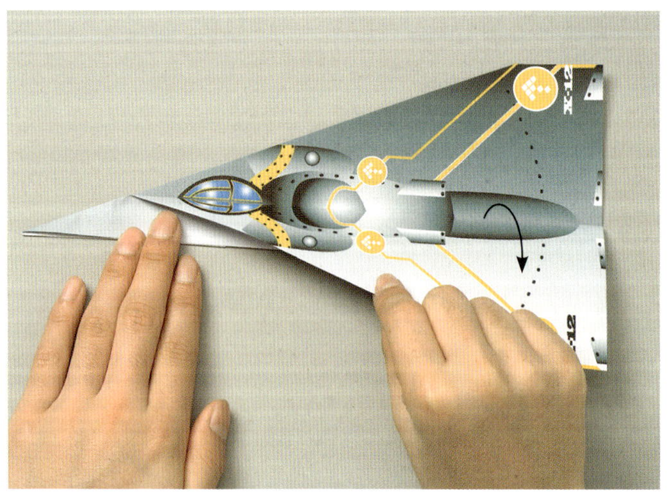

2 Turn over the wing, making the fold along the line of the cockpit so that the designs on both sides of the plane match.

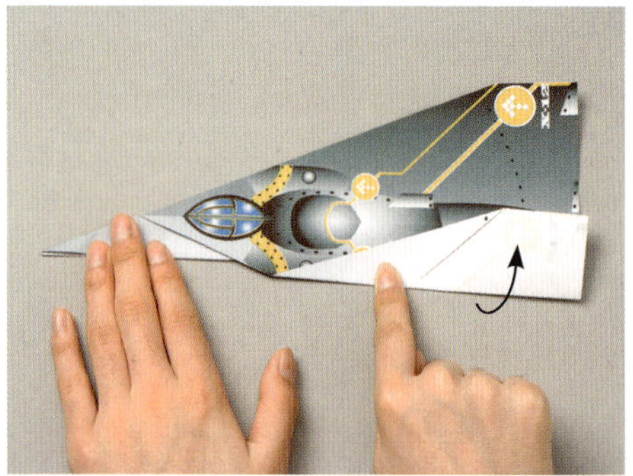

3 Fold back the outer half of the wing, starting the fold line at the edge of the design at the front.

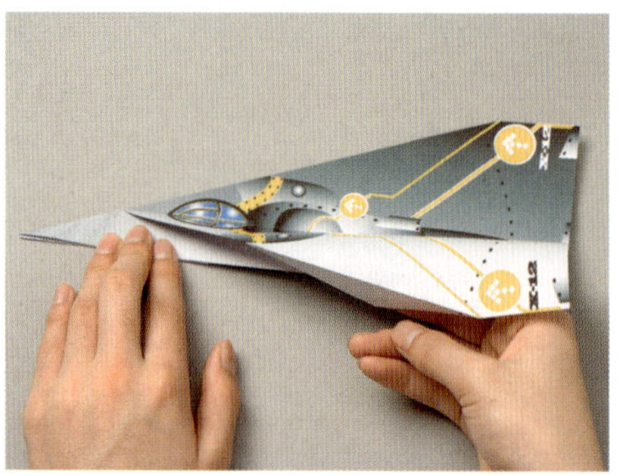

4 Reopen the flap and lift the entire wing, opening out the flap underneath with your fingers.

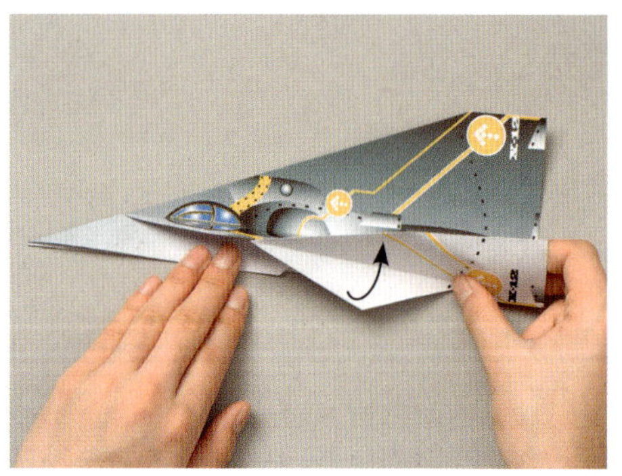

5 Reclose the wing, reversing the diagonal crease.

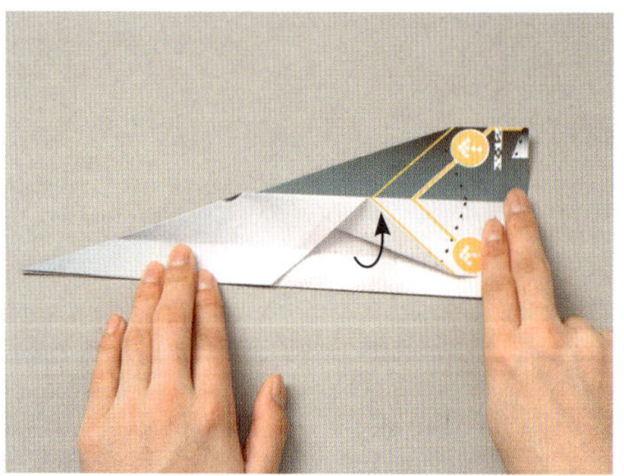

6 Press the wing flat against the other side of the plane and check the folds match the photograph.

7 Holding the end of the wing in your fingers turn it upward until the angled edge sits snugly against the inside of the earlier crease. Turn the object over and repeat steps 2–6 on the other side.

8 Make a long, shallow angled flap at the base of the back of the plane.

9 Open out the plane and reverse the crease from the previous step so that it sticks out above the plane as a tail fin.

12 BLUE BIRD

This plane is reminiscent of a bird, so we've created a sweet paper design for it. Throw it gently without using much force, letting the bird catch the breeze with its long, sleek shape. Get together with friends and make enough blue birds to create an entire flock.

Skill rating ● ● ●

You will need

1 sheet of A5 (8¼ x 6in/21 x 15cm) paper

1 Fold the paper in half lengthwise before opening out to leave a crease. Next fold in the corners at one end so that they meet along the central crease.

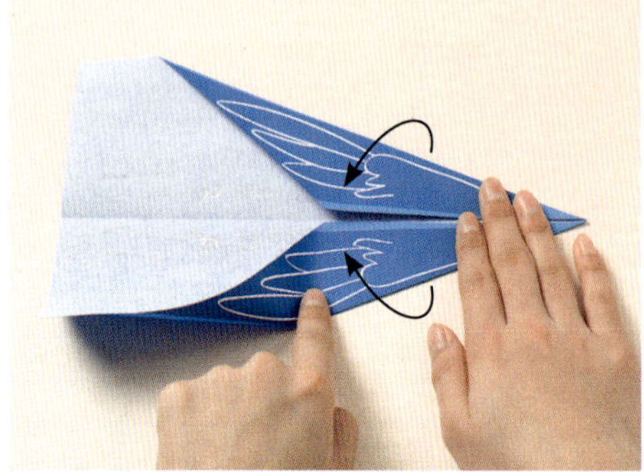

2 Fold in the angled edges so that they also meet along the center crease line.

3 Fold the object in half then turn the nose upward at a shallow angle about 3in (7.5cm) from the tip to make a crease.

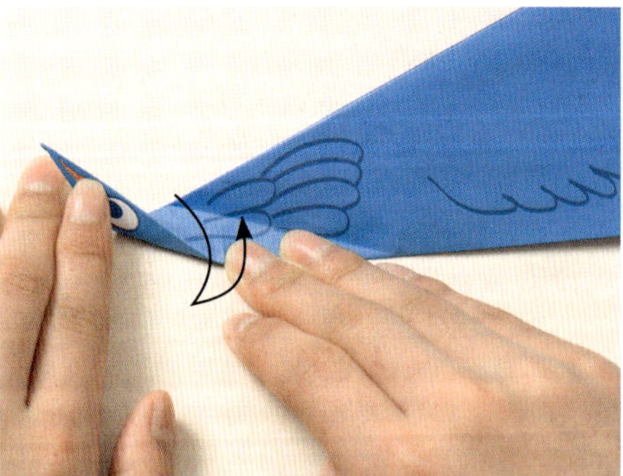

4 Open out the nose then fold it up again at the same angle as before but this time about 2in (5cm) from the tip.

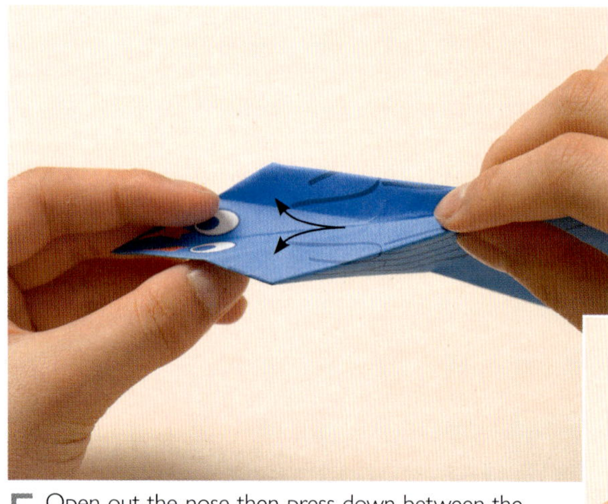

5 Open out the nose then press down between the two digaonal folds to reverse the crease and refold it.

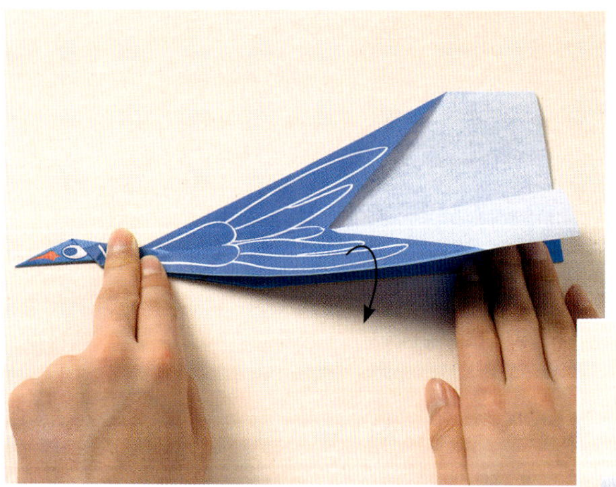

6 Fold down the wings so that the creases are parallel to the base of the object.

13 BRICK

Make your friends laugh with this comedy airplane—they definitely will have never seen a brick wall glide effortlessly through the sky before! At first glance you'd think the Brick plane shouldn't stay in the air because of its weight and clumsy appearance but in fact it defies all logic and flies really well.

Skill rating ● ● ●

You will need
1 sheet of A5 (8¼ x 6in/21 x 15cm) paper

1 With the printed side up, fold the paper in half widthwise to make a crease and open out. Next fold one end into the center and then fold the same side in half again.

2 Fold the paper in half crosswise but do not make a crease. Just press down the near point to mark the center and open out.

3 Turn over the folded corners, using the center mark made in the previous step as the fold point, ensuring that the sides match.

4 Turn up the wing tips using the folded corners as the marker points. Now your Brick is ready to fly! See page 11 for tips.

14 FLYING FISH

The flying fish skims over the surface of the sea, leaping over the waves, almost like an airplane flying over water. By swimming with great power it can break through the water into the air, using its momentum to make a seemingly unending series of jumps. And the sleek lines of this plane successfully replicate the grace and agility of the fish.

Skill rating ● ● ●

You will need

1 sheet of A5 (8¼ x 6in/21 x 15cm) paper

Paper glue

1 Make a crease along the middle of the paper then it open out and fold the corners at one end into the center.

2 Now fold the tip back so that the point lies on top of the folded corners and make a crease.

3 Turn the nose back and open out one flap before turning the tip of the object back in. This will begin to reverse the folds of the flap.

4 Reverse the diagonal crease against the main sheet of paper and bring the point down so that it lies on the central crease.

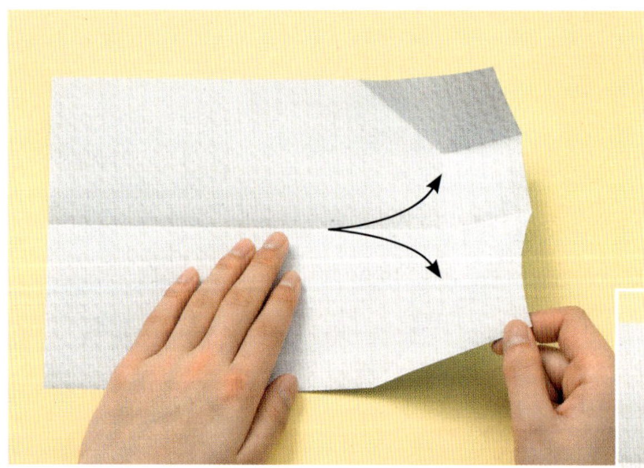

5 Open out the entire sheet. Reverse the creases on the other side and fold both sides back in together.

6 Turn over the folded end of the paper, making a crease along the edge of the previous folds.

7 Fold both corners in so that they meet in the middle of the edge folded in the previous step.

8 Close up the paper along the central crease and turn down the wings.

9 To keep the plane's shape, dab some paper glue along the inside of the body and press together.

15 JUMBO JET

The jumbo jet is one of the largest passenger planes and seeing it immediately brings to mind dreams of flying away to distant lands and wonderful vacations. This plane is made from a paper with designs of the jet repeated in every direction—when it is complete, let your imagination take you off to exotic beaches or snowy mountains.

Skill rating ● ● ●

You will need
1 sheet of A5 (8¼ x 6in/21 x 15cm) paper

1 Fold the paper in half widthwise and open out then turn the corners along one side in so that they meet on the central crease.

2 Next turn the tip back so that it sits on the far edge of the paper.

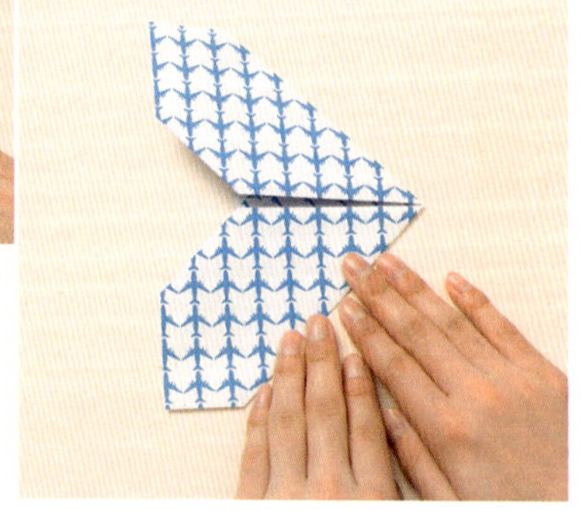

3 Fold the far side across at an angle from the center mark so that the front edge lies along the central crease, then repeat on the near side.

4 Lift up the near half of the object then fold back the wing about 3/8in (1cm) up from the main crease. Turn over and repeat on the other side.

5 Fold back the wing tips to finish.

USEFUL INFORMATION

Origami paper is available at most good paper stores or online. Amazon and eBay are good sources for paper, or try typing "origami paper" into an internet search engine to find a whole range of stores, selling a wide variety of paper that can be delivered directly to your home address.

USA

HOBBY LOBBY
www.hobbylobby.com

MICHAELS
www.michaels.com
TEL: 1-800-MICHAELS (1-800-642-4235)

UK

HOBBYCRAFT
www.hobbycraft.co.uk
TEL: +44 (0)330 026 1400

JP BOOKS
www.shop.jpbooks.co.uk/en
TEL: +44 (0)20 7839 4839
E-mail: info@jpbooks.co.uk

JAPAN CENTRE
www.japancentre.com/en
TEL: +44 (0)870 820 0055
E-mail: enquiry@japancentre.com

THE JAPANESE SHOP
www.thejapaneseshop.co.uk
TEL: +44 (0)1423 876320
E-mail: info@thejapaneseshop.co.uk

WEBSITES

Mari Ono: www.mari-ono.com
Origami Club: en.origami-club.com
OrigamiUSA: www.origami-usa.org
British Origami Society: www.britishorigami.org

INDEX